THE
INEVITABLE GUEST
A Survival Guide
To Being Company & Having Company
on
CAPE COD

THE INEVITABLE GUEST

A Survival Guide
To Being Company & Having Company
on
CAPE COD

Marcia J. Monbleau

MARCIA J. MONBLEAU

COVER & ILLUSTRATIONS
by
LUCRETIA ROMEY

Acknowledgements

Some good friends have helped a great deal with this book, one way or another. For suggesting, reading, proofing, encouraging and often goading, I'm deeply grateful to: Pat, Nancy C. and Nancy S., Mary Ann, Carla, David, Pam E. and Pam H., Lynne, Eric and Margy. And my thanks once again to Kevin, for his computer skills and for making me laugh.

For additional copies of *The Inevitable Guest*, kindly send $11.95 per copy (Massachusetts residents, add 5% tax) plus $2.50 for shipping and handling to:
Marcia J. Monbleau
14 Old Tavern Lane
Harwich Port, Mass.
02646

Bog House Press

Fourth Printing

ISBN 0-9676220-1-8

*To the Oldtimers,
a wondrous breed
with strong hands, good humor,
big hearts and small houses.
We miss them.*

Contents

Final Thoughts from One Who Lives Here

In the Beginning

Once upon a time, when life was simpler, a woman of the Nauset tribe knelt by a cook-fire near the beach. Her husband walked out of the forest, carrying a piece of bark with marks on it.

"Got a letter from your cousins," he called out. "They want to come down the last week in July, first week in August."

"No good," the woman said, stirring something in a pot. "That's when your parents are coming."

Foreword

There are, generally speaking, five sorts of people
found on Cape Cod at one time or another:

native residents,
natives who are not residents,
residents who are not natives,
summer residents who are natives
and summer residents who are not natives.

A sixth classification, frequently seen with all of the
above, is the group known as "guests." Guests are not to
be confused with "tourists," who come for a few days,
stay at motels and never share toothpaste with any of
the first five types.

Native residents have had company all their lives, as
have summer residents who are natives. These hosts are
fairly casual about guests, seeing them as a natural and
inevitable part of any year—like ticks. Visitors come and
go with tide-like regularity, and folks just sit a little
closer on the couch.

Residents and summer residents who are not natives,
however, may suffer what might be called a Period of
Adjustment. Everyone they ever knew from wherever

---◆---

they used to live wants to "come see the new place." Guests arrive and depart in a constant flow, leaving their hosts with barely enough time to shift the sheets.

It might be a good idea to talk over some things so everyone knows what this visiting business is all about and how to share time, space, food and bathrooms in an agreeable sort of way.

This little book, intended for hosts and guests alike, is offered with affection for all and malice toward none. It is written by someone who belongs in Category #3 and who just one time—many years ago—was a guest.

On "Stopping By"

Few words are more frightening to a Cape Codder than "stop" and "by," particularly when used together as in the following example:

"We've been in Maine for two weeks, and we thought we'd like to stop by on the way home."

It's time to look at your map. Draw a line from Maine to Alabama, one from New Hampshire to Virginia and another from Gloucester to Newark. Do you see Cape Cod anywhere along those lines?

The correct answer is "No."

Cape Cod is not "on the way" to anyplace. It is a "side trip," "day trip" or "wide loop," but nobody stops by "on the way."

So what does "stop by" mean to the Cape Codder who has made the mistake of answering the phone? Are these people "stopping by" for lunch? The day? A swim? The month? 'Til school starts?

People "stopping by" usually are vague. "We're not sure when we'll get there. We're just taking it easy." That's a bad sign. "Taking it easy" may mean they have no deadline and can stay until Columbus Day. "Don't make any special plans," they say. "We just want to see you."

"Making no special plans" involves a lot of planning.

First off, the about-to-be-hostess can't leave the house, because she doesn't know when people are going to show up. Will she need luncheon meat? Is there enough bread? What about supper? Will they have eaten? Are the sheets dry yet? Should she make a quick dump run? Is the bathroom presentable? Does the dog still smell skunky?

Anyone planning to "stop by" should consider the hostess and walk a mile in her sneakers.

A suggested phone call is as follows:

"We'll be there by 11. We want to take you folks out for lunch, but we have to be on the road no later than 2:30."

"Why, sure! Come on down!"

What to Wear

When packing for a Cape Cod vacation, check the tags on your clothes. Don't bring anything that says "dry clean only" or "wash separately in cold water, spread out and pat dry." The label should read, "Whatever."

Pack light, but not so light that you have to do a wash every fifteen minutes. Most Cape houses have septic systems in the back yard, and all the stuff that gets piped out winds up there. It does not flow to some city sewer system that's so far away you forget the "stuff" was yours to begin with. So we think twice about making "stuff," and that includes laundry goop. (Other "stuff" comes from kitchen sinks, showers, bathtubs and toilets.)

Bring clothes for hot weather, warm weather, cold weather and rain. (That's one day.) Bring your own beach towel; a big old blanket is good, too. And a hat, for the fair of skin, faint of heart or thin of hair.

Bring t-shirts, including one dark one that may be worn repeatedly and won't show lobster squirt. (See section on lobster.)

Fashion tips for men: don't bring slacks with whales or yacht flags on them (some people here already have them, and they look silly); never wear brown or black socks with sneakers or sandals; wear plain shirt with plaid shorts, plaid shirt with plain shorts but never a plaid shirt with plaid shorts. Finally, plaid and checks never are suitable together.

Proper attire after sundown is what you had on all day, but with a sweater.

Proper attire for dining out will vary, depending on whether dinner is clam strips or veal marsala. In all cases, however, men with brown socks will be seated near the kitchen.

Sometimes, suggested dress is "Cape Cod summer casual." This means you will put on something just a little nicer than beach duds. Look for ladies in pink and lime-green dresses and men in yacht flag pants.

Children's clothing should be basic, mix-and-match, wash-and-wear or, if money is no object, disposable. Children are dirty. You can send a boy off to a violin lesson, and he will come home with gravy in his belly button. The dirt possibilities on Cape Cod are endless: beach dirt, dead horseshoe crab dirt, bike dirt, dog dirt, bird dirt, garden dirt, bug dirt, mildew dirt, food dirt, popsicle dirt and just plain dirt.

The best outfit for a child is one in which he can be hosed down.

Kid Stuff

If more than two days of rain are expected during the week, urge your guests to leave their children at home. Presumably they will be putting the dog in a kennel or leaving their cat with food on the floor and an open window. See if they can make either of those arrangments for the children.

However, guests with infants should be encouraged to bring them. Children who are not yet ambulatory are welcome in most places. They arrive in a tote bag, can be placed on the floor and are unable to move. As long as you don't step on them they're quite pleasant to have around, and you have proven yourself to be child-friendly.

Keep in mind that this policy is good for one year only. By the time another visit is planned, the immobile infant will be crawling or, worse yet, walking. So plan ahead. Sometime in mid-winter, let your friends know (in the nicest way possible) that they are welcome to bring their child back as soon as he/she is old enough to mow the lawn. For the sake of friendship, offer to provide them with a list of motels, camp sites or resorts in the Adirondacks.

Sometimes children happen in the best of families, and toddler or pre-teen guests cannot be avoided. Parents must remember that not everyone's house is "child-proof." Your hosts should not have to hang their treasures from the ceiling before you arrive. Rather than expecting a "child-proof house," parents ought to bring a "house-proof child."

Children of average intelligence are delightful company. They can be placed in front of the television, with some pretzels perhaps, and will stay there until they fall asleep and tip over. Your hosts are free to go about their business, confident that the child will not do experiments in the kitchen, tie the dog's tail to a chair or back the car into Gramma Alice. The same principle holds true at the beach. A nice ordinary child will paddle about until his lips turn blue and will make so many trips back and forth from the water yelling "Mommy, watch me!" that he will eventually pass out on the blanket.

Parents of precocious children should stay in a motel where they don't know anyone.

Finally, parents ought to be particularly sensitive if their hosts are either childless or single. Despite what he or she may say, no single person wants to play any sort of board game with a five year-old.

Cape Codders who have guests with children during a week of bad weather—or as we like to call it, "a damp spell"—should turn immediately to "Rain, Rain Go Away" on page 69.

Having said all that, it must be admitted—however reluctantly—that some children are quite nice people, and may turn out to be agreeable company.

Creature Comforts

Figuring out what to do with/about visiting children is a stroll on the beach compared to dealing with a dog or cat. Look at it this way; if your hosts really like animals, they probably have one or two of their own. If they don't, they don't. Unless you are very close friends, and your host is godfather to your Schnauzer, leave the dog at home. You are going to a house that doesn't have hair on the sofa, drool on the kitchen floor or land mines all over the lawn. Bringing your hair, drool and poop is not appropriate.

This holds true even if your hosts do have pets. A resident dog or cat doesn't understand a home invasion. Some strange critter is sniffing around his home, nosing into his bowl, sleeping on his bed and decorating his yard. If the Cape Cod dog misbehaves, gets cranky or tries to chew off the tail of the visiting cat, he will be punished.

Doesn't seem fair. Leave pets at home.

If these warnings don't convince you, consider this; Cape Cod has sand fleas—big, mean, indestructible ones. Did you know they can live in a carpet for a year, even without a host animal? If you bring Spanky to the Cape, you may have many more passengers on the way home.

On the opposite side of this delicate issue, hosts must

consider the sensitivities of guests who aren't used to and don't care for pets. You adore Buster, but Aunt Ruth might be startled by a wet nose up her skirt while she's napping on the verandah, and Jack from your Navy days doesn't want cats padding across his face in the middle of the night.

Be sure to work out all potential conflicts ahead of time.

Guests in a house with resident pets should ask about and abide by the rules. "Don't let the dog out" probably means "Don't let the dog out," so don't do it. He may disappear for three days, eat the neighbor's roses again or turn over the garbage can and find those deadly chicken bones. A house cat may be de-clawed, so close the door behind you when you leave.

Never make your own rules for somebody else's pet.

But Seriously, a note to both hosts and guests. If you think you're doing your dog a favor by taking him/her to the beach with you, think again.

Hot sun, burning sand, salt water and bugs can add up to a miserable, even fatal, outing.

The sun you crave is your dog's most dangerous enemy. Dogs can't sweat, and they overheat easily. They should never be on the beach between 10 am and 4 pm. If you must take your beloved pet along, out of some distorted notion of companionship, make sure he has enough shade. Rent an umbrella, if you have to; don't assume he'll get adequate protection in the shade of your beach chair.

If you have to hop across hot sand, remember that your pet's feet are equally sensitive. Worse yet, a dog will often lick his burned foot, swallow sand and make himself sick.

If you still insist on hauling him along, keep an eye on him. If he begins to pant heavily, if his sides heave or if his tongue turns deep red or purple, he may be in the early stages of heat prostration. Act fast to prevent brain damage and death. Cool him immediately by dousing him with water or wrapping a wet towel around him. Feed him ice cubes, or have someone run to the ice cream truck. Do NOT give him unlimited water; he could drink himself to death.

If you think your dog is having a high old time romping in the surf, keep in mind he won't feel as swell later on. Salt water may kill fleas, but it also dries out the skin and aggravates itching problems.

And don't keep throwing the stupid ball into the water for him to fetch, particularly at a beach where there's surf and an undertow. A dog, out of loyalty, will continue trying to please you even when he is exhausted.

Just because a dog has a coat doesn't mean he can't get sunburned. Short-haired, shaved or close-trimmed dogs are very susceptible to burning and to torment by insects at the beach.

Still determined to take your beloved pet with you? Check first. Many Cape towns do not allow dogs on the beach. If you get there and find that Bubba is not welcome, do NOT leave him in the car for the day.

It all boils down to this; your dog may give you that heartbroken, sad-eyed look when you leave the house, but he'll then find a comfy place and take a snooze. And when you come home with a burn, itchy skin and bug-bites, he'll be waiting—cool, protected and safe.

We're Here!

Hosts expecting company should peek out the window when they hear a car pull in. This will give them an opportunity to collect themselves in the event they don't recognize these people from a hole in the wall.

While helping unload the car, the woman host will ask the woman guest how she is, how the kids are, how long the trip was and did they stop along the way. She then should say, "I imagine you'd like to stretch out for a bit. You must be exhausted."

The man host will ask the man guest some things about how the car went, what kind of gas mileage he got, which routes they took and how the traffic was at the bridge. Then he says, "Come on in and put your feet up, fella. You must be worn out." But first, "Why don't you pull your car right over there."

The children guests will tumble out of the car and run screaming toward the resident dog, who will crawl under the porch and growl for the first time in his life.

On entering the house, the woman guest says, "This is beautiful. I love it!" and the man guest says, "How 'bout those Red Sox?"

Guests should now go straight to their room and stay there for at least an hour. They can unpack, freshen up or lie down, but they should stay there.

This will give everyone a chance to talk about everyone else behind everyone else's back, giving everyone an idea of what everyone is in for.

After this short break, the real visit begins.

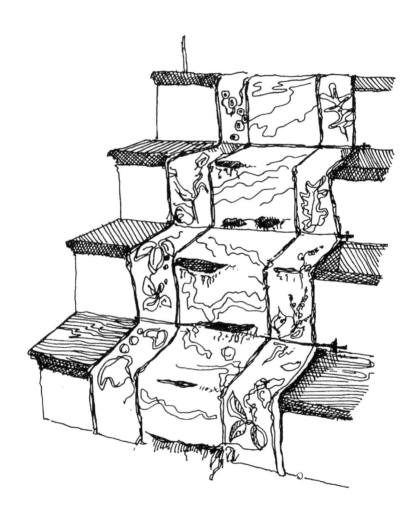

Good Night, Sleep Tight...

Travelers wishing to have matching queen-size beds, private bath and tv with remote are urged to stop at a nice motel. Once having made the decison to not do that, they should graciously accept whatever their hosts offer by way of accommodations.

If the guest room were the biggest, sunniest and most convenient room in the house, it would be called "the master bedroom." The guest room is small, with twin beds, and if there's any room for your clothes in the closet you're not on Cape Cod.

In old Cape houses, "quaint" and "hazardous" are interchangeable. Be careful while here and decide ahead of time that whatever happens, you will not sue.

Here are some things to watch out for.

Great Aunt Betsy's hooked and braided scatter rugs are on the guest room floor. They are old and valuable, and your hosts love them. But notice they are not in the master bedroom. Get out of bed slowly, plant your feet firmly and make no quick turns, else you will shoot across the room and out the window.

Toilets sometimes are fitted into awkward spaces under the eaves, along with tubs and showers. Before taking a bath, note that the ceiling slants dramatically above the tub. After that nice, end-of-day soak, stand up slowly to avoid a concussion.

Old Cape Cod stairways are, in other parts of the world, called "ladders." Allow extra time for going up and down. Turn slightly sideways, place your weight on the balls of your feet, grip the railing, mind your head and watch out for the scatter rug at the top.

Some antique houses—Half-Capes, Three-Quarter Capes and Full-Capes—were built at a time when the tallest man in town was 5' 7". Remember to duck when going through doorways or coming down the stairs.

These are just a few quaint features of authentic Cape houses. You will discover others during your stay.

Consider this: you are indeed fortuntate to be occupying that little guest room. Otherwise, your hosts might be getting $75 a night for it. A true Cape Codder with a spare room under the eaves often is known as an "innkeeper."

Your room may be small and the floor-covering deadly, but you will sleep better than you have in months. You'll come down the ladder the first morning and say, "I was out like a light. I didn't move all night!"

It has something to do with salt air and tides and the moon and the way the earth turns and the fact that your room isn't costing you anything.

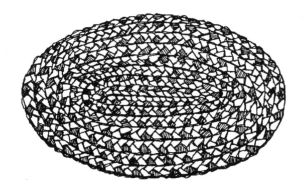

Don't Let the Bedbugs Bite

Most Cape Cod hosts and hostesses have, from time to time, heard from the guest room (or the bathroom, or living room, or almost anywhere) a scream, followed by the word "Cockroach!"

There are a few differences between The Cape and New York City, and this is one of them. Chances are, you did not see a cockroach.

We have two special bugs here, and although one of these bears a very slight resemblance to the city critter, it is not, not, NOT a cockroach, but an earwig. You may find an earwig curled up in your sneaker, in the underwear drawer, under the edge of a towel or trying to avoid being sucked down the bathtub drain. It is harmless.

The earwig is from the order "Dermaptera." It is small, very slim, with antennae and a pair of forceps on its behind.

The cockroach, from the order "Blattaria," is an important bug with a song written about it—"La Cucaracha." As far as we know, there is no music having to do with earwigs.

The second local bug is defined as a "Wood Louse," which sounds disgusting. Its more common name is "sow bug," and it, too, is harmless. Oddly enough, you hardly ever see a live one. Sow bugs just seem to be dead all the time. Dead ones in the corner. Dead ones under the radiator. Dead ones behind the recliner. Sow bugs are small and oval, and they can move fairly quickly. Mostly, of course, they're not budging. They're dead.

There's no need to scream if you see earwigs or sow bugs. Most important, don't assume that their presence is proof that your hostess is a slovenly housekeeper.

Earwigs and sow bugs are simply—here.

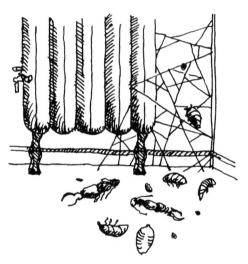

Occasionally, depending on weather and wind direction, there will be "yellow jackets" on the beach. Defined as a "small, social wasp," the yellow jacket's goal in life is to eat your lunch, particularly if it contains something sweet. If you have a peanut butter and jelly sandwich, for example, the yellow jacket will land on the bread and ride right into your mouth if possible. A good trick is to put a half-can of sweet soda in the sand about 10 feet away. This will attract the wasp, leaving you to dine in peace. Maybe.

Keeping it all Together

The invitation to "make yourself at home" has certain limitations. Your hosts are delighted to have you here, but they really don't care to see your toiletries. Nobody wants to find your nail-clippers on the coffee table.

A general rule of thumb is that guests' belongings should be kept within a three-foot radius of their bed. This includes wet sneakers, soiled undergarments, dental floss, deodorant, nasal spray and anything having to do with hair removal.

There are two exceptions to this rule—postcards (in the process of being written) and books. Guests may leave books—particularly this one—anywhere.

If visitors are to keep their stuff together, hosts must free up some dresser space and surfaces in the spare room. (To determine how many empty drawers are needed, multiply the number of guests by the number of days they're staying. Then divide by four.) Empty the contents of those drawers (Christmas wrapping paper, scrapbooks, bits of wool, etc.) into a carton, along with family photos from the dresser top, and place carton in the garage (out of the way of mice).

Your hosts have been kind enough to make available some dresser space for your use. However, if you want drawers that actually open, it is recommended you bring

a bureau from home. Cape Cod drawers (in dressers, desks, hutches, sideboards and in kitchens) slide open two days a year—usually on a dry weekend in November.

The procedure for opening any drawer on the Cape is as follows: take hold of the two pulls or knobs, begin a rocking, side-to-side, pulling-pushing motion and have someone stand behind you to break your fall when the thing finally lets go.

Should you, by some brilliant maneuver, get those drawers open, leave them that way during your stay, else you may have to go home without your undies.

Guests who don't know any better may bring dress-up outfits that need to be hung in a closet. There are, rumor has it, three empty closets on the Cape, but nobody knows where they are. In an effort to be accommodating, however, hosts should remove a few things from the guestroom closet. This project will require three family members and some type of prying device.

Finally, it's thoughtful to provide a towel rack in the guestroom. Wet towels will dry in anywhere from two hours to four days, depending on the weather. If everyone's towels are left in the shared bathroom, a nice crop of mushrooms will sprout behind the commode (next to the dead sow bugs).

Another word about towels. Odd as it may seem, Cape Codders feel that a drop or two of water on a towel does NOT make that towel filthy and in need of immediate washing. After bathing, guests are encouraged to hang up their towels to dry, rather than pitch them into the washing machine. Presumably, any dirt that might have tainted the terrycloth went down the drain.

Out of consideration to your hosts (and their septic system), remember that a wet towel is not a dirty towel.

For I, who hold sage Homer's rule the best,
welcome the coming, speed the parting guest.

Alexander Pope
1688-1744

What's That Smell?

This is a question heard often from vacationers who are not familiar with Cape Cod. There are any number of answers, depending on the time of day, wind direction, what month it is and how close you are to a clam shack.

But, for the most part, the correct answer is "mildew."

Mildew came to Cape Cod on the Mayflower. English by birth, it made its home here and prospered. With its cousins, must and mold (Pilgrim spelling, "mould"), it likes paper, cloth, paint and leather. Many years ago, mildew went to Arizona, but nearly died and had to fly home in a carton of old National Geographics.

Mildew is found anywhere there is dampness, and vice versa. Go back to your map again, and see all the blue around Cape Cod. That blue is extremely wet. It's good for fishing, swimming and boating, and it keeps your skin soft. But it makes smelly on your books.

Anyone allergic to must and mold might consider another vacation location. Otherwise, remember that the smell has nothing to do with your hosts' housekeeping habits, so don't sit around the house for a week holding your nose.

As a related aside here, if, while lying in bed, you notice a slight buckling in the ceiling above your head, rest easy. National Geographics have been accumulating in the attic since 1947. We don't dare throw out any of them, in case someone has to do a report on Tasmanian devils or Zimbabwe.

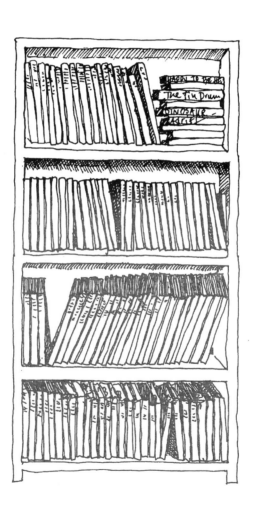

Where's the Beach?

Everywhere.

While traveling to Cape Cod, study your map. Notice that the Cape is shaped like an arm. Provincetown is the fist. Chatham is the elbow, and Falmouth is the pit. So to speak. Notice, again, all the blue around the arm. That is water.

Here's where it gets tricky. Not all of that blue part is ocean. The blue at the bottom is Nantucket Sound, or—off Falmouth—Vineyard Sound and Buzzards Bay. The top blue is Cape Cod Bay. The blue at the right is the Atlantic Ocean.

What difference does that make, you might well ask.

Not a bit.

Unless you want to swim.

If you need to know all about tides and currents and depths and related temperature fluctuations, buy another sort of book. This one provides the following information:

Sound water on the south side of the Cape is warm. Cape Cod Bay water is cold, and Atlantic Ocean water is so cold your bathing suit may crack.

Here's more:

Tide changes along the Nantucket Sound shore are not dramatic. In other words, there's always water in

which to swim, high tide or low. However, at low tide on Cape Cod Bay—in Dennis, for example—your swimming water is somewhere in Maine. It will be back later. In the meantime, enjoy a lovely walk on the flats. (Flats is a word meaning "sand without water.") But it's a good idea to stroll parallel to the beach. If you walk straight out for a long, long way, you might lose track of time and distance and the water coming back from Maine will sneak up on you.

In addition to floating ice cubes, the Atlantic shore can have the biggest waves on Cape Cod and a strong undertow. Undertow means this—if you are standing in the water, and a big wave comes in, your top half will be pushed toward the beach. Meanwhile, an underwater force in the opposite direction will yank you off your feet and halfway to Portugal.

Being in water must be taken seriously anyplace. It must be taken very seriously on the Atlantic side.

Believe it or not, some people think salt water is itchy, seaweedy and filled with crawling, pinching, grabbing, biting things. It is. So Cape Cod also has lots and lots of freshwater ponds with good beaches. The only crawling, pinching, grabbing, biting things you'll find there are wearing bathing suits and eating chips.

Visitor, you may go to any public beach anywhere on Cape Cod free of charge. Unfortunately, your car may not. If you can walk to a beach, fine. If not, you'll need a beach sticker for parking privileges.

Each town has its own fee system, and the cost varies depending on the town and the length of your stay here.

Perhaps your hosts will let you take their car (with a resident sticker) to the beach for the day. More likely, they will prefer to drop you off there and come back to pick you up when they're darned good and ready.

Parents, wherever you go beaching, remember one thing; the lifeguard is not your babysitter.

After about 5 o'clock in the afternoon (and any time after the summer season), you can go to public beaches on the Cape with or without a sticker. You won't get a sunburn, but the best of the rest of it is there in all its glory, and the boomboxes have left for the day. Take a swim, take a hike, stay late enough to watch the sunset and see why a lot of Cape Codders think this is the best time of day.

The Herding Instinct

City-dwellers coming to the Cape take a deep breath, stretch their arms wide and exclaim how wonderful it is to be in wide open spaces, far from the madding crowd, away from the crush of the subway, free of the sidewalk masses and the ear-splitting din of it all.

Then they do the oddest thing.

They go to the beach first thing in the morning and sit down within four feet of the only other person there—a lone woman who is halfway through *Anna Karenina*. They spread blankets, set up chairs, raise umbrellas, un-hitch the pre-schoolers, turn on the boombox and begin making calls on their cell phones. (Please see "Techno-No-No.")

This behavior is the result of living in overcrowded conditions for a long time. These folks don't get away from home; they bring it. Rather than loving open space, they are terrified by it. It's lonely and unnatural, and there might be a vacationing mugger running amok on Craigville Beach some morning in July.

Moreover, they don't want to hear all that Quiet, so they bring their own noise and make some more, turning the music way up and then hollering over it.

Soon the children are amusing themselves by running across other people's blankets and throwing stones at

seagulls. They're told to "go play someplace else," which turns out to be at the feet of the woman who is reading.

Beach etiquette is simple:

Resist the impulse to "herd" or play "space invaders." Find your own place, and try to keep your personal noise within that area. Headphones are a lovely invention.

Keep track of the kids. You love them, but nobody else does.

Communicate with your children up close and quietly. Don't let them get 60 feet away and then screech back and forth. No one else cares to hear, "Keviiin, you need sunscreeeeen!!"

See that your umbrella is grounded securely, and pay attention to it if the breeze picks up. A sudden gust could turn it into a spear.

And at the end of the day, just before you pick up your blanket to snap off the sand, check the wind direction. Make sure what you dump doesn't go in your neighbor's face.

Marketing Strategy

The man stood there, frozen like a bunny in the head-lights of an oncoming car. He stared. He read. He pondered. He was, in short, an accident waiting to happen.

He got rear-ended. Luckily, there were no real injuries. The man's heel was treated at the service counter, and he was released.

This wasn't the first time there had been a pileup there. And it won't be the last, unless something is done and done now—before anyone else is hurt.

In the winter it's bad enough, but in summertime the situation is critical.

It's time to speak out—to both guests and hosts.

With all due respect, retired men should NOT accompany their wives INTO the supermarket. There simply isn't enough room for people who don't know what they're doing. Our stores already are crowded, and if you add a wandering, staring, cart-pushing husband to every wife, well, it's just not working. She's been doing the shopping on her own for 30, 40, maybe 50 years. Once the kids grew up, she flew solo, making her list according to aisles, never having to double-back. Up-and-down, zip-and-zap, over and out.

Now she has this BIG kid tagging along. Chances are he was C.E.O. of Something or Other, Inc. and extremely capable, we hasten to add. But he spends 20 minutes staring at bread, and in fruits and vegetables he's a menace.

Worst of all, the Chairman of the Board wants to walk NEXT to his wife, not in front of or behind. That's against International Supermarket Law. If you walk two abreast, what happens to oncoming traffic? And if he stops to look at the wide variety of salsas, he leaves his cart in the middle of the aisle—sideways!

This perfectly nice man cannot be permitted to take up space, dawdle, compare beet prices and come to unexpected stops in front of toilet tissue. That's when accidents happen.

Therefore, we offer a modest proposal.

What if supermarkets were to set up some sort of, say, Play Group in a corner of their parking lots? They could provide chairs, newspapers, maybe a chess board, and, of course, other retired men. This would provide an activity while freeing up the aisles and simplifying the shopping process.

So, to guests and hosts alike, please do walk the beach together, stroll the main street together, sit at the band concert together and snuggle up together in the movie theatre.

But please, sir, don't go food-shopping with your wife. There just isn't room.

Whose Vacation is it, Anyway?

Cape Codders may go to Nova Scotia, Maine or New Hampshire in the fall, or to Florida or Barbados in the winter, but they do the oddest thing about summer vacation; they don't have one.

They're hunkered down, working to bring home the bacon bits and trying to maintain their routine while summer guests whoop and holler and parade around in plaid shorts, singing "Summertime, and the Livin' is Eeeezy."

No, it isn't. It's business as usual. More business than usual would be even better.

Remember this when you land with suitcases, Margarita mix, fishing tackle, tennis raquets and the clarinet you're determined "to take up again" while on vacation.

No thank you, your hosts don't want to watch late-night television and swap stories from high school until the wee hours. They have to get up when the clam crows, so let them go to bed. And they have first dibs on the bathroom in the morning.

They'll try to take a little time off while you're here, maybe go to the beach with you one afternoon, and, yes, dinner out some night would be lovely.

But don't make them feel guilty about working. They

have to, so they can go to Sarasota in January and send a postcard to you—in Buffalo.

Disregard all of the above, however, if you are visiting some retired friends. They'll be ready to run you ragged.

Which brings us to the flip side of this matter. Hosts have some responsibilities, too.

First off, this is your guests' vacation. Don't overplan for them. Say, for instance, they've just driven from Chicago with three children and a sweaty uncle, spent two hours getting over one bridge or the other and had trouble following your directions to 10 Codfish Lane. Consider the possibility that they'd rather not crawl right into your car for a nice tour of the area before the sun goes down.

It's a swell idea to discuss in advance whether visitors want to see and do a hundred things while they're here or just lie on the sand and think about whether the clouds look like lambies, duckies or frying pans.

And if your guests are looking for night life and want to whoop it up, that's fine. Let them go. You can turn in early.

But don't forget to leave a light on and the door unlocked.

Is The Air Conditioning On?

It might be if we had some, but we don't so it isn't.

No matter how hot it might be while you're here, it's worse where you came from or you probably wouldn't have left. Turn on the weather channel, notice that it's 102 degrees in Atlanta and stop asking about air conditioning.

For approximately three days in August it would be nice to have a cooling system in Cape houses. But your hosts, ever mindful of the fact that they pay one of the highest electric rates in the USA, don't think a few miserable nights warrant sticking one of those ugly boxes in a window. They are willing to tough it out, wear their birthday suits to bed and sleep on top of the covers.

You should do the same—follow suit, as it were.

Things will be back to normal soon, and you'll be asking where the blankets are.

For the time being, stop asking about air conditioning. Open a window.

A cautionary note: You may notice that Cape Codders have a lot of stuff on the window sills, between the panes or hanging from the locks: glass fishies, antique cup plates, stained glass, crystal prisms—anything that looks pretty with sunlight shining through. So, just because there are windows in your guest room doesn't mean they can actually be opened without some advance planning.

On Touring

Guests, do not be afraid to venture out on your own. It will give you privacy to talk about how lumpy the beds are and how that little roughneck of theirs could use some manners. At the same time, it will provide your hosts with a chance to do a wash, put their feet up and try to figure out what they ever saw in you to begin with.

A day spent apart is a blessing for all.

Remember one thing; you cannot get lost on Cape Cod. If you go too far in any direction, you'll drive into the water.

The Cape is divided—for no particular reason—into four sections: Upper, Mid, Lower and Outer. This has absolutely no bearing on anything, unless you're looking at the What-to-Do Section in the newspaper where events are listed according to area—or should be. There are no hard and fast rules for this, but the Upper Cape is nearest the bridges—Falmouth, Sandwich, and so forth. The Mid-Cape is about where you'd expect it to be—in the middle—including Barnstable, Yarmouth and Dennis. Harwich, Brewster, Chatham and Orleans generally are thought of as the Lower Cape, and Eastham,

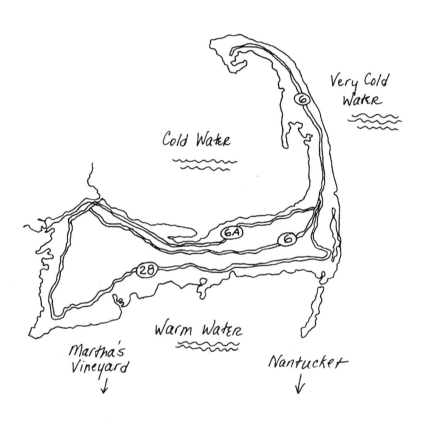

Very Cold Water

Cold Water

Warm Water

Martha's Vineyard

Nantucket

Wellfleet, Truro and Provincetown are out there on the Outer Cape.

Note: Hyannis is NOT a town, but one of the villages of Barnstable. Hyannis also is not, as has been suggested, the capital of Cape Cod.

There are three main roads on the Cape, until the Orleans/Eastham rotary, after which there is one main road for the rest of the way.

The main main road is Route 6 or the Mid-Cape Highway. It goes along the center of the Cape and will get you from the Sagamore Bridge to where you're going in fairly quick order. But you will not see one single thing, not a clamshell, shingled house, sailboat, retired person or fisherman. And because some very smart people passed a "no billboard" law a long time ago, you won't even know how far you are from Stuckey's or South of the Border. What you will see are exits, pitch pines and stubby oak trees. Period. The Mid-Cape Highway is not Cape Cod, any more than Route 95 is Virginia.

If you want to see signs—enough to choke a whale—drive along Route 28, which will take you from the Bourne Bridge all the way to Orleans. This is the road that snakes along the south side of the Cape. Some of it is pretty, ah, un-quaint, but if you want shoes, t-shirts, hardware, miniature golf, gas, gifts, inflatable alligators or a fast burger, it's a very good place to be. And if you've been on the main drag of Myrtle Beach, South Carolina recently, Route 28 is quite lovely.

When 28 hits Harwich, there is a noticeable decline in inflatable alligator shops. From Chatham on up to Orleans, the road passes harbors, coves, cranberry bogs and beautiful Pleasant Bay. Finally, in Orleans, Route 28 bumps into Route 6A (you haven't read about that yet) and disappears altogether.

Note: The Commonwealth of Massachusetts people who put up state road signs on Cape Cod don't know north from south. A sign may say "Route 28 north" (because the road turns that way eventually), when you know perfectly well you're headed east. Not to worry. Follow the route number, and pay no attention to which way they say you're going.

Also, please keep in mind that "28" on a sign refers to the route number, not the speed limit.

The purist may choose to travel along Route 6A, which parallels the Mid-Cape Highway on the north side and goes from Sandwich to Orleans, where it meets Route 28. Then they both disappear, and become Route 6 again. This final stretch runs clear to Provincetown, and some of it is three lanes, so pay attention and drive very carefully if you want to see that lumpy bed again.

But back to 6A. This is the road where all the postcard pictures are taken: captains' houses, white clapboards and weathered shingles, old roses and tall steeples. But Route 6A is not for those who want to get somewhere fast. Right in front of you, a nice couple from the midwest is going 20 miles per hour, moseying and gazing and talking about how cute everything is. There is virtually no chance to pass. So take a deep breath, simmer down and prepare to meander.

Route 6A is the Old Kings Highway. It must be noted, however, that if they wanted a quart of milk, some shock absorbers or an inflatable alligator, the old kings probably went to Route 28.

"Meanderers" are the people driving very slowly on Cape roads. "Meanderees" are the ones stuck behind them. "Meanderers" are vacationing on Cape Cod, and being on vacation means you don't have to get up early, wear a tie, go to work or use the rear-view mirror or directional signal.

If you are meandering along Route 6A and see a red-faced person behind you with steam coming out of her ears, chances are she is a "meanderee." She lives here and is on a half-hour break from work to get a filling replaced. Meanderers are encouraged to put on the directional (before braking, if at all possible) and pull off to the side of the road long enough to let that woman with the toothache be about her business. Meandering may be resumed immediately thereafter.

If rambling guests want to see the water, there's a sweeping generalization that holds true more often than not; take any road that goes south off Route 28, any road that goes north off 6A or any road that goes left or right off Route 6 (after Orleans).

Just wander. You won't get lost.

Wet maybe, but not lost.

We agree that if you've come from Newark or Chicago or Washington, D.C., the towns here look awfully little and the streets are sort of dinky. You might even call them insignificant. Nonetheless, please do NOT make U-turns on Main Street, whatever village you're in. It's thoughtless, dangerous and too arrogant for words.

If the visitor learns nothing else from this reading, remember the following; as you drive around the Cape, you will cover a lot of ground in a short time and have a happy experience if YOU NEVER TURN LEFT. That is to say, if you are at a stop sign and want to turn left onto a main road, you will sit there until horses have kittens. No matter where you want to go, TURN RIGHT. Get onto the main road, go up a bit, turn left off it and swing back. Go around the block, if you must. Go to the next town, if necessary. Go over the Sagamore Bridge and around the rotary, for heaven's sake! You may drive five miles out of your way, but will get where you're going ahead of time as long as YOU DON'T TRY TO TURN LEFT!

No guest can stay three continuous days without becoming an annoyance.

Plautus
254-184 B.C.

A Sign of the Times

Guests moseying around the Cape may notice an abundance of "For Sale" signs. This is a quaint local custom that had its start in 1872.

Winter that year was tough. The harbors froze solid, fishing was off and a lot of hardworking folks were running short of the food they'd put up the previous autumn.

It was down in Chatham—or maybe South Yarmouth—one Sunday when Benjamin Doane—or was it Eldredge?—or Cahoon?—got talking with some friends, most of whom were in the same boat, so to speak.

Well, Ben told the men he was near desperate and was going to sell his place—the old house his father had built in (or about) 1809. He figured it was worth around $750, a good sum then, it being a sturdy house with solid chimneys.

So the sign went up late that hard winter, and people from the mainland started passing by, even slowing down. Before long, Ben was taking offers, good ones, too, far in excess of his asking price. Ben and his wife, Dorcas, were vastly entertained for a few months and forgot how cold and hungry they were.

The harbors thawed out, mud ran thick in the roads

and life was on the upturn. Ben planted his peas. Roses started to bud. Fishing was good.

Benjamin Doane (or whatever his name was) never sold the house. But he felt quite good just knowing he could have—and for a lot more than it was worth.

To this day, when winter is too long and life is on the hard side, "For Sale" signs sprout here and there around the Cape.

Folks aren't really planning to sell.

But they're more than willing to listen.

Thanks Just the Same

Unless you are a longtime friend and frequent visitor who is very familiar with the premises, do not offer to cook dinner. It's much too tiring and confining for your hostess. She must stay within earshot to answer all the questions you holler from the kitchen.

Q. Where will I find a really BIG pot?
A. I'll get it. It's in the garage, under the Christmas ornaments.
Q. Do you have tongs?
A. In the drawer next to the stove.
Q. Got 'em. No, don't get up. I see vinegar. Do you have RICE Vinegar?
A. No. Do you need it?
Q. Ummm, no. I guess I can make do. Where will I find the garlic press?
A. In the drawer next to the stove?
Q. Same drawer? No, don't get up. Got it! I found your brown rice. Do you know it really should be refrigerated?
A. Do you want me to get a new box?
Q. Ummmm, no. I guess this will be ok. Where will I find the Extra Virgin Olive Oil?
A. In the refrigerator.

Q. Where? No, don't get up. Ah-ha. Got it. It was on the door.

A. I know.

Q. Do you have any arugula?

A. I don't know. What is it?

Q. Never mind. How about Rosemary?

A. Rosemary who?

Q. Where will I find a really small pot?

A. In the drawer under the stove.

Q. That's a funny place for it. When was the last time you had your oven calibrated?

A. Why?

Q. No reason. What time do you want to eat?

A. We usually eat at 6.

Q. Oh. Umm, this won't be ready 'til 8:30. Is that ok? No, don't get up.

If you truly want to give your hostess a special treat for dinner, the best thing you can make is reservations. If you want to give her a very special treat, you go out to dinner. She'll stay home and curl up with scrambled eggs and toast.

"Stay" is a charming word in the vocabulary of a friend.

Louisa May Alcott
1832-1888

Dining—The Ins & Outs

"Where's the best place for Seafood Fra Diablo with nasturtium garni?"

"Who knows. I live here. I don't eat out."

That exchange may be heard often on a Cape Cod porch at twilight. Visitors who arrive smacking their lips and planning to chew their way from Woods Hole to Provincetown must remember that their hosts haven't the time, energy or wherewithall to join you. They're saving all those things for their own vacation sometime after Labor Day.

Moreover, when they do eat out, it's pretty basic. Your hosts probably cannot point you to nouvelle cuisine. They know plainelle, friedelle and cheapelle.

Generally speaking, Cape Codders are a meat-and-potatoes lot. They like iceberg lettuce, mayonnaise, graham crackers, cold cereal, pickles, coleslaw, most fruit, macaroni and cheese, baked beans, ice cream, anything in the chocolate family, all forms of potatoes, Eastham turnips and peanut butter. Recently, they have converted to the "all beef" variety of hotdog, while maintaining that those with unspecified ingredients really do taste better.

Seafood is defined as clams, oysters, scallops, mussels, lobster, sole, flounder, cod, swordfish, haddock and scrod—sometimes spelled "schrod"—which is simply young haddock or cod.

Snapper, Mahi-mahi, dolphin, Mako shark and grouper are not real fish; they come from foreign waters, like off Florida, and could not possibly be fresh.

Your hosts most likely do not cook, eat or recognize anything having to do with the following words: tahini, tabouli, hummus, tempeh, shitake, couscous, cilantro, cumin, tofu, ginger, turmeric, cardamom, carob, matzoh, wasabi, escarole, artichoke, kabob or ratatouille.

They seldom, if ever, grind, saute, marinate, sprinkle, press, mince, julienne or "arrange" things on plates with little dribbles of sauce around the rim.

What they do is boil, fry, roast, mash, stir, soak, crumble, slice, peel, scoop and scramble. Their spice cabinet contains salt, pepper, cinnamon and some oregano they bought when you were here two years ago. For added zip, ketchup is on the refrigerator door.

Your hosts will provide you with good food that will stick to your ribs, probably for a long time.

And there are enough restaurants of every stripe and nationality (including American) to satisfy your yen for eating out. To find out what and where the best ones are, spend a day on the beach and ask other visitors.

Finally, if you all are good friends/relatives—and if you're not, why are you here?—make breakfast a do-it-yourself meal. Hosts should find out what their guests like, have it on hand and explain where things are. Guests may then get up as late as they wish, fend for themselves and clean up afterwards.

Lobster

When Miles Standish first visited the Cape from Plymouth in 16-something-or-other, he approached the first person he saw and said, "Is there a good place here to get lobster?" Since then every guest has asked the same question, sometimes substituting the word "cheap" for "good."

Once and for all, lobster is not "cheap." Here. There. Anywhere.

That settled, there are two good places for lobster on Cape Cod—out and in. In is best.

Guests might offer to buy lobster for dinner some night. Your hosts probably haven't had any since last year's company was here. Then go to the fish market, pick out what you want and ask the folks there to cook it for you.

This way your hosts will not have to hear—for the thousandth time—"Oooh, you're not going to kill it, are you?! Oooh, I can't bear to watch!"

Lobsters—around here anyway—almost never commit suicide. If you are reluctant to kill something, cabbage would be a good meal.

The dirty deed being done by someone else, it's time to set the table. Cover the whole thing with newspaper. If you, like many other guests, insist on getting *The New*

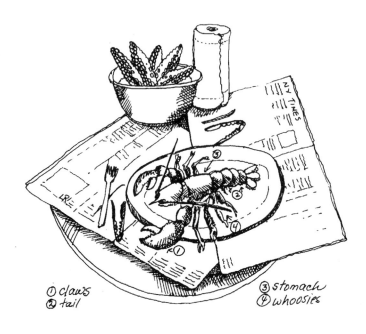

① claws
② tail
③ stomach
④ whoosies

York Times while you're here, this is the best use for it—
all of it—except the glossy magazine section, which is
non-absorbent and therefore completely useless.

Put great big bowls in the middle of the table.
Alongside, put some Cape Cod napkins (paper towels).
Get out picks and nut-crackers and forks. Add a platter
of corn on the cob and two bags of potato chips.

There you have it.

Salad and wine are optional, but no vegetables, for
heaven's sake. And never milk.

Ready? There are four basic parts to a lobster: the

claws and arms that connect them, the tail, the stomach (up toward the eyes) and those little whoosies that flap off to the sides. Claws, arms and tail make excellent eating. Some people like to suck on the whoosies. While doing this, they roll their eyes and squirm, maybe to make you think they're getting something really good, which they're not.

Finally, very few people are hungry enough to root around in the stomach. You can spend an extra half-hour scraping and poking there, but what you end up with looks like a pile of wet, gray sawdust. If someone else at the table likes that sort of thing, give him your stomach.

The lobster may contain a lump of red stuff or green slimey stuff. The red is roe, or eggs, the slime is lobster liver, called tomalley (not to be confused with tamale), and the discovery of either will make most visitors draw back, shudder and say "Ick" twice. Pass it over to someone who likes liver 'n eggs, or throw it away. (That's what the big bowls are for.)

Don't ask the host to crack open your lobster. Figuring out how to do it is part of the fun.

You are eating at home, as we have suggested, because this is one messy meal. Despite everyone's best efforts, lobster water and bits of shell will be flying around the room, and puddles of goo will collect on the Times. It also is the loudest meal. When was the last time you heard people giggling, grunting and shrieking, "Oooh, I don't know how to doooo this" while eating pork chops?

When finished, remove plates, tools and shell bowls from the table. Roll up the newspaper, and take it to the dump—immediately, if possible.

You can go "out," of course, order "lazy man's" (or "lazy woman's") lobster and let someone else do all of the above.

But "in" is better.

Wheelies

One of the nifty things to do on the Cape is ride a
bike. You rode one when you were a kid, so why not?
You never forget. Your hosts have two bikes in the shed,
but the tires have been flat since 1971. So you'll go to
the rental place, and in twenty minutes be wobbling
down Route 28 with everyone else in brown socks.
Then you'll hit a patch of sand and....

What? You didn't have sand along the side of the road
in Cleveland when you were little?

On Cape Cod we've moved sand out of the way just
far enough to put down a road. There are almost no bike
lanes anywhere, and many summer drivers have enough
trouble finding their way around without having to keep
an eye on rent-a-bikers.

So stay off main thoroughfares. The Cape has some
terrific bike paths. Find the Cape Cod Rail Trail, for
example, and you'll be happy as a clam and twice as safe.

Here are some tips for beginning bikers, along with
questions most often asked.

•Carry money and aim for a store where they sell ice
cream and nachos. This provides a goal, and if you
schedule your tour properly you can ride for 20 minutes

(going and coming) and have a 45 minute "rest stop" in the middle.

•When you get to a corner, remember to put on the brakes before getting off your bike.

•Do not turn to look behind you while riding. Turning your head to the left causes a simultaneous steering to the right and vice versa. You will end up in a cranberry bog.

•Buy a rear-view mirror. It will help you prepare for the possibility that the driver bearing down from behind is an acquaintance who will toot "Hi" at you just as he passes. If you are ready for this, you will not ride up the nearest utility pole.

•When on a long ride, remember to bend your elbows from time to time. Otherwise, someone else will have to feed you dinner.

•If you're a novice biker, wear a helmet.

•When you get to be an experienced biker, wear a helmet.

Q. Where is the safest place to ride on Cape Cod?
A. On your porch.
Q. Is it all right to take my hands off the handlebars?
A. If you belong to an HMO.
Q. What happens if I put on the front brake but not the back one?
A. Show me what you mean. I could use a laugh.
Q. How do I keep dogs from nipping at my heels?
A. Wear spurs.
Q. What's better on a long ride, a front-pack or back-pack?
A. A six-pack.
Q. Is it all right to wear headphones while riding?
A. Yes. That way it will come as a complete surprise when you're hit by a cement truck.

The Shell Game

A new law has been enacted, and enforcement will begin early next summer. Everybody leaving the Cape will be stopped, all cars searched, and the following question asked; "Are you taking any seashells over the bridge?"

Those answering "No" will be sent back to get the pile they left on the front stoop.

It's time to get tough about this.

Every year thousands of things are picked up by thousands of guests, and nobody ever takes anything home.

It begins innocently enough. Adults do it. Adults tell kids to do it. "Why don't you go down by the water and pick up some shells, sweetie?" The second half of that sentence, unspoken, is "and leave me alone."

Cape Cod does not have a particularly unusual assortment of shells—just the basics: clams, scallops, slipper shells, along with egg cases, seaweed, dead horseshoe crabs, other little bodies and a lot of rocks. Folks who live here don't pick up anything, but people from, say, Kansas, think that whatever washes up on a beach is pretty darned exciting.

So it goes. The pile on the front stoop, back porch or guest room dresser gets bigger—and stinkier.

Favorite things for visitors are shells still occupied by

something. They're fun. "Well take this home, and clean it out." But with the first whiff—after the creature has died and baked in the sun for a day—the thrill is gone.

We agree. Those shells would look pretty glued around a picture frame. They'd be darling stuck to a little jewelry box or put in a glass lamp. We wouldn't do any of those things for the world, but we think you ought to. Just take them. All of them.

But it's the same story every summer. The car is loaded. It's time to leave. Becky whimpers. "Mommy, I forgot my shells." Mommy says, "Oh, honey, we haven't got room. We'll get more next year." What Mommy means is, "We're not going to have that smell in the car all the way home."

That's all right, Becky. As your hosts always tell Mommy and Daddy, "If you've forgotten anything, we'll mail it."

Note: Empty seashells make nice souvenirs, but those that are occupied should be left alone. Someone's alive in there.

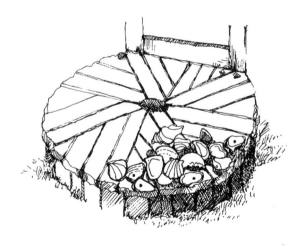

Shot But Sweet

The fastest way to spot a foreigner (anyone from beyond the bridge) is to listen as he orders those little round things that come broiled, baked or fried. "I'll have the scaaaallops," he says, and right away you know he can't tell low tide from high. Practice now. Scallop, as in wallop. "Scall" is like tall, ball, fall or call.

Next is "Falmouth." One "L." Now feel free to stretch that "A," as in pal or gal.

Chatham is "Chattum," but Eastham is "East-ham," for absolutely no good reason.

"Quahog" is pronounced "ko-hog." That's that.

And on Cape Cod in the summer, you'll find two kind of shots: Bermuda shots and shot shots.

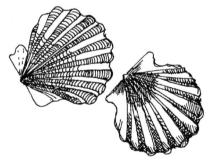

---◆---

Company, villainous company, hath been the spoil of me.

William Shakespeare
1564-1616

The Theory of Relativity

Folks who come to the Cape on holiday sometimes bring along thick skin and some attitude, possibly because they live in places that have made them acquire those things along the way.

If you live in The Big City, for example, you might have become accustomed to shrieking for a cab, being testy with postal clerks, demanding service from a cranky waitress or talking in a very loud voice to someone who doesn't seem to understand you.

If that behavior works where you come from, fine. But your hosts will be most grateful if you don't bring it over the bridge.

Keep in mind that the people who are providing you with B&B (as well as L&D) live here. They know the postal clerk by name, along with the mailman, vegetable-arranger, checkout lady, pharmacist, and the woman who cashes their checks at the drive-in window. They get along with all of these people because they want to and because it makes things a little nicer. And if you think that's very small-town, it gets more so.

Remember when you got cross about the price of limes the other day? Remember standing in the checkout line and telling everyone around you how "outrageous" prices are here? Remember the 16 year-old clerk you snapped at?

Her mother is your host's sister's husband's cousin.

Your host's nephew's wife is the waitress you were rude to, and her mother is the bank teller who said she could not cash your personal check from Detroit.

The Cape Cod Theory of Relativity is as follows; everyone is related by birth, marriage, work or church affiliation, so watch what you say.

Cape Codders, no matter where they travel, tend to treat waitresses, busboys, chambermaids and store clerks with respect. There's a simple reason for that; most of them spent their high school and college summers as waitresses, busboys, chambermaids or store clerks. They are not comfortable when their houseguests treat the waitress like a bar-wench.

Finally, you may be accustomed to yelling over subway noises and other city racket, but you needn't holler at Cape Codders. They're not hearing-impaired.

They're just ignoring you.

Techno-No-No

When one ponders the past, it's hard to imagine how humans of a hundred or more years ago survived and prospered, what with being so out of touch and all.

Men on whaling ships left home knowing they would not see it again for a year or two. Cape fishermen headed out to sea for months at a time. It took weeks to get a letter, days to ride the horse to Boston and hours to race around town looking for the doctor when a baby was due.

How did they manage?

What did they have to make them feel important?

With what could they annoy the bejeezus out of everyone around them?

Would the Revolutionary War have ended sooner if George Washington had owned a cell phone?

Answers to these historical questions remain a mystery, but we rather like the concept of having all cellular phones confiscated at the bridges and held there until departure. Short of that, lifeguards, church deacons, store owners, librarians, theatre ushers, airline hostesses and anyone waiting in a public line for anything ought to be deputized, given cute little badges and authorized to snatch any such phone from the hands of loud people.

Or it could be sort of a Wyatt Earp system. "We don't

allow no cell phones in this here town, pardner. You can pick it up when you ride out."

In the event none of the above solutions is possible, we must throw ourselves at the feet of cell phone showoffs and beg for some consideration.

Please don't use them in public places. Please turn off the ringer in social settings. Don't make calls while in libraries, bookstores and other places where silence is cherished. Please don't talk ten times louder than you do on your home phone; we honestly don't care if you have a broker, an agent or a producer. And for the sake of all of us, please don't make calls while you're trying to navigate in traffic around here.

If Cape Cod hosts think the above is intended for guests only, they're wrong.

Cellular phones undoubtedly are good to have in a crisis, but we're glad historical emergencies had to be handled without them.

We're sure, for example, that Longfellow would not have been inspired to write, "Listen, my children, and you shall hear of the midnight phone call of Paul Revere."

Where the Gulls & the Cantaloupe Play

Guests may bemoan the fact that their hosts are too busy to spend much time with them. Take heart. Your hosts almost certainly will invite you to enjoy with them a getaway to one of their town's most fascinating places, where you can take in the great outdoors, watch wildlife and see other genuine Cape Codders in their natural habitat.

Sadly, these magnificent sites are fast-disappearing, so you would do well to visit one of them as soon as possible. You won't see their like again.

Fortunately, for residents and visitors alike, each town has one. So pack up the wife and kids, turn on the car radio and have a jolly ride. And while you're at it, take the garbage.

The authentic Cape Cod dump is going the way of all good things. Once upon a time, "dump-picking" was a popular year-round outdoor sport. Folks took stuff there, and other folks brought it home. They sanded it, painted it and put it in the living room.

Then people in high places said we couldn't pick the dump anymore. A lot of Cape Codders haven't had new furniture since.

Then they said we couldn't call it a "dump" anymore. It became the "landfill," and now most towns have a "transfer station."

One by one, Cape "landfills" are being "capped." That means they're covering up all the goop once and for all, planting tulips and having lawn parties there.

But if you move fast and are lucky, there may still be a feeling of the good old days.

Hosts, take your guests; they can see piles of rotting wood in one place, twisted metal in another, rusty refrigerators here and brown Christmas trees over there. Those old cedar shingles would be great for kindling, but don't try to take any. They don't do a full body-search for dump-picking, but they might slap you around a little.

Because all household refuse has to be bagged and dropped into a container, you can't see garbage these days. And, sadly, the seagulls have about given up. The dump no longer is their restaurant. Perhaps they'll find a new home. But what of local politicians? Where will they campaign once Cape Cod is dumpless?

Go now, before it's too late.

Take the garbage.

And have a nice day.

*Withdraw thy foot from thy neighbor's house, lest he be
weary of thee and so hate thee.*

Proverbs

Rain, Rain, Go Away

Your hosts are Not Responsible for the Weather.

That being said, let's all keep in mind that we have to put up with the weather, whether there's weather or not.

Sulky company makes for edgy hosts. No one wants your holiday rained out, least of all the people who have to listen to all that muttering and whining.

On a good day, New England has the best weather in the world. That perfection is appreciated all the more because of oogy days in between. The Cape has pea soup fog, rain, black clouds and gale force winds; later the same day it has blue sky, silky ocean and perfumed air. What it does not have are tornadoes, flash floods, six-month droughts, sandstorms, earthquakes or 150 inches of snow in the winter.

Remember that when you get blown off the beach by a nor'easter.

A couple of soggy days are nice. They give guests the chance to go shopping, catch a movie, track water into museums and play that "How Many Out-of-State License Plates Can We Count" game on Route 28.

Similarly, a rainy patch gives hosts time to stay home, snuggle in, relax and do some of the things that get

pushed aside when the beach beckons or their guests are underfoot.

With rain thrumming on the roof and gushing from the downspout, Cape Codders can reorganize the top desk drawer, re-grout the shower, trim edges off coupons, line up canned goods according to food groups, put last year's vacation pictures in an album or loll around in their bathrobes eating things with high fat content. They can scour, polish, dust, doze, sort through old magazines, straighten out shoes on the closet floor or put the nozzle on the vacuum cleaner and suck up spiders in the cellar.

Notice that all this home activity is possible only if guests have left the building.

This is the rule: if it's nasty out, that's where guests should be. Hosts and their company must not be under the same roof for any length of time during a week-long damp spell.

However, if it's extremely damp—say, like in a hurricane—you may be forced to spend quality time together.

Hosts might suggest some activities to keep everyone in a pleasant frame of mind. Perhaps the group could sit in the bedroom and watch sheets mildew. If it's really, really windy out, light a fire in the fireplace and count how many seconds it takes for the living room to fill with smoke. Take five jigsaw puzzles, put all the pieces in one bag, shake them up and then do the puzzles. (You are not allowed to look at the pictures.) Have each person try to guess what the dog smells like. This list probably will include things like old tires, wet mittens, athletic socks and damp chickens.

Hosts are urged to be creative and have on hand plenty of paperbacks, videos, coloring books, popcorn and anti-depressants.

Of course one of the very best places to go on a rainy day is the beach. More than likely you won't have to pay, and there will be lots and lots of parking spaces.

No matter what effort hosts make, their guests will remain convinced that this is some plot to ruin their vacation, that it is raining only on Cape Cod and raining hardest of all right on this very house.

They could be right.

Funny You Should Ask

"Heavens! What do you do around here in February?"

Chances are, your host has heard that question before and is a mite tired of it. Chances are you could be the last straw. He may even sit you down, waggle a finger in your face and say something like:

"Listen, Bub (or Missy), we do plenty! Let me tell you about February.

"First of all, the reason that so many things seem to be closed in the winter is that there are so many things to be open in the summer! The things that close have a darned good reason to! Miniature golf courses are a little nippy in winter. Outdoor trampolines get brittle, and three times around a go-cart track'll give you a chapped face.

"Here's a list of a few things open in February: food, clothing, hardware, video and drug stores, flower, gift and antique shops, movie theatres, restaurants, bowling alleys, gas stations, places to get your hair cut, your teeth fixed, your tires rotated and your tickets to Aruba.

"Here's what else: libraries, churches, schools, homes and offices.

"So you might say that in February we have what most other places have.

"One more thing. The beach never closes.

73

"Sure, we have winter weather. But it's a little less hostile than in some other places. And there's one thing we don't have. Black snow. You get your black snow in Boston and New York. It freezes in gutters and won't go away. After three months, it smells. We get white snow down here, Bub, and not much of it, either. Around here, all you need to get rid of snow is a broom, a few hours of sunshine and a salty wind off the water.

"And the other thing is, February's short! It's quiet, too. We can drive from one place to another without getting stuck behind the likes of you!

"We're pretty fond of February. Look at it this way; one of the things that makes July so great is—February."

Aren't you glad you asked?

Estimated Time of Departure

Social customs differ remarkably from region to region. In New York City, for example, if you are leaving an apartment after a visit, your hosts will slam the door on your backside. You walk to the elevator alone, hail a cab alone and go to the airport, also alone. Your hosts consider that their responsibility ends at the apartment door.

Not so in New England, where we tend to dawdle. Your hosts will carry suitcases to the car and stand there helpfully while you cram everything in.

You'll all go back to the house to scout around for things forgotten. Exiting again, everyone will sit down in lawn chairs to talk for a few minutes. Then you'll slap your thighs, stand up and say, "Well, we hate to go, but...." Your hosts will slap their own thighs, stand and say, "Well, we hate to have you go."

That may not be absolutely true, of course, but it's what people say at a time like this.

Once you're in the car, you'll roll down all the windows and keep talking. In fact, it's likely you will talk more now than you did all week. This final spurt of conversation is, in part, triggered by guilt. Everyone wants to make sure that everyone still likes everyone, despite all that business about air conditioning, mildew, what the dog did in Aunt Sally's beach hat, forgetting to turn off the stove, breaking the dresser drawer and taking too many showers.

It is not unheard of here for hosts to actually lead their departing guests to the Mid-Cape Highway. Although it may appear to be a way of making sure they leave, it is simply a thoughtful gesture.

Hosts should make this departure process as easy and swift as possible. Guests are not expected to strip their beds, wash the sheets, repair the dresser or have the cesspool pumped before leaving.

The exact time of departure is important. If you announce that you will be leaving at 10 o'clock in the morning, do so. A good rule of thumb is, start your engine within 15 minutes of when you said you would.

If you wake up on your day of departure and see the sun shining for the first time all week, you may want to take one final swim or pick up a few last-minute gifts. You're certainly entitled to do that.

But you cannot come back to the house.

That Hostess Gift

After you get home, do not send a thank-you gift that is inappropriately expensive—like a television or greenhouse. It will make your hosts feel uncomfortable. Worse, they will feel compelled to invite you back year after year. Making them feel obligated was not your intention when sending a gift.

Was it?

Also, it is unsuitable to send a gift to replace something that you consider old, inadequate or ugly. "We thought this beautiful electrified kerosene lantern would look lovely on the end table." That is poor etiquette; your hosts may be very fond of their lava lamp. Similarly, sending new sheets would seem to indicate that you think their bed linen is nasty and you don't want to sleep on it the next time around.

Refrain, too, from sending something that you've decided would improve their living conditions. A dehumidifier comes to mind. Cape Codders like being clammy and having a gray-blue coating on their shoes.

And while we're at it, don't wander out onto the porch while you're here and say, "You know, I found this really great rug cleaner at home. I bet they have it here."

Why not send a simple thank-you note, along with a

box of little lavendar soaps shaped like scallops. Nobody likes them or knows what to do with them, but they will never give offense.

HostSpeak, GuestSpeak

It's a known fact that Yankees in general and Cape Codders, in particular, don't mince words—ordinarily. When talking with their guests, however, they may hold back just a bit—for the sake of politeness, and it's more than likely that visitors do the same.

Every now and then, folks say one thing when they're thinking something else. It goes like this:

Host: "Was there much traffic?"
(We didn't expect you this early.)

Guest: "That's such a pretty bathing suit."
(Isn't it the same one you had last year—and the year before?)

Host: "Don't worry, sweetie, he won't bite."
(For the hundreth time, leave the dog alone.)

Guest: "Do you have Starbucks on the Cape?"
(Your coffee tastes like soap.)

Host: "We're going to the drugstore. You need anything?")
(Why didn't you bring your own shampoo?)

Guest: "We'll pick up a few things at the grocery
        store."
        (We need pumpernickel and some deli.)

Host: "I guess your kids got a little over-tired at the
        beach."
        (In about two minutes, I'm going to smack 'em!)

Guest: "We want to take you out for dinner."
        (No more beans and hotdogs, please.)

Host: "We'll close our door tonght, so our reading light
        won't bother you."
        (You snore like a buffalo.)

Guest: "Where's a good place to use my hair dryer?"
        (How come there's only one outlet in the
        bedroom?)

Host: "Well, did that shower feel good?"
        (You used up all the hot water.)

Guest: "I just love all your collectibles!"
        (Don't you ever dust?)

Host: "What time do you folks have to get away
        tomorrow?"
        (How soon are you leaving?)

Favorite People's Favorite Places

By now it's clear this is not a guide book to Cape Cod. That was never its purpose. Chamber of Commerce booths in all the towns have enough pamphlets and maps to wallpaper the Pilgrim Monument, and for one-stop shopping visitors can browse at the Cape Chamber of Commerce just off Route 6 in Hyannis.

What is included here is a list of places that some Cape hosts always want to show their guests or, even better, send them off to see on their own.

So, without rhyme or reason, and in no particular geographical order, the favorite places and activities of a few friends are as follows:

The Brewster Mill and Herring Run, any Cape Cod Baseball League games, The Cape Cod Rail Trail, water taxi rides to Monomoy Island (for picnics or seal-watching), Hyannis Harbor cruises, band concerts anywhere and everywhere, the Herring River Conservation area in Harwich, whale watching out of Barnstable Harbor or Provincetown, Sturgis Library in Barnstable (the oldest in the country), the old Spiritualist Campground in Harwich Port, Great Island in Wellfleet (for walks and picnicking), the Sandwich Boardwalk (at both low and

high tides), Kelley Chapel and the Capt. Bangs Hallett
House in Yarmouthport, Heritage Plantation in
Sandwich, Spohr Gardens in Falmouth (especially at
daffodil time), anything at the Cape Museum of Natural
History in Brewster, including the John Wing Trail,
Chatham Light (at sunrise)and the Chatham "cut," Rock
Harbor in Orleans (at sunset), Nobska Light (Falmouth),
Nauset Light and beach (Eastham), Highland Light
(Truro) and any other lighthouse you can find, The
Cape Playhouse and Cinema in Dennis, the cranberry
exhibit at Brooks Academy in Harwich Center, ferries to
Nantucket and Martha's Vineyard (from Harwich Port,
Hyannis and Falmouth/Woods Hole), antique shops and
art galleries on every corner, South Cape Beach
(Mashpee), Old Indian Burial Ground (Mashpee),
Nickerson State Park (Brewster), the Flats (northside
beaches at low tide), Woods Hole Oceanographic
Institute and The Marine Biological Laboratory in
Woods Hole (visitor centers and tours), Fort Hill in
Eastham, the boardwalk at Bass Hole in Yarmouthport
(at both tides), the Harwich Junior Theatre, the Atwood
House Museum/Mural Barn and Josh Nickerson's beach
camp (Chatham Historical Society), The Nob at Quissett
Harbor in Falmouth, the Sandwich Glass Museum,
Pilgrim Monument & Museum in Provincetown, the
Thornton Burgess Museum and Green Briar Nature
Center (both in Sandwich), the Cape Museum of Fine
Arts (Dennis), the Pairpoint Glassworks at the canal in
Sandwich, Long Nook Road in Truro, East Dennis vil-
lage, everything at the Cape Cod National Seashore
(Visitor Centers at Salt Pond in Eastham and Province
Lands in Provincetown), Scargo Tower in Dennis, Uncle
Tim's Bridge in Wellfleet, Woods Hole Science
Aquarium, any historical society museum, Brooks Free
Library in Harwich, Route 28 from Chatham to Orleans
along Pleasant Bay, Race Point in Provincetown, any

Cape cemetery (for artistry, poetry, history and occasional humor) and any back road to anywhere.

For more information about this or that, just ask around. And if you've found your own favorite places that aren't on the above list, there's a page at the end of the book for jotting them down.

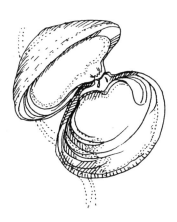

You Probably Didn't Know This, But...

Few people realize that Cape Cod's Cranberry Bogs, until about the turn of the century, were, in fact, huge forests of cranberry trees that rose thirty to forty feet in the air. For years, the crops were harvested in a most difficult and time-consuming manner. Workers gathered the fruit by one of two methods. They climbed great ladders and dropped the cranberries into large gunny sacks held by co-workers on the ground, or they wielded "berry-pickers," tiny little scoops fastened to the end of 30-foot poles, a system that required keen eyesight and the shoulder muscles of a draft horse.

Needless to say, the harvesting took weeks, and by the end of that time much of the crop had turned to mush.

In 1837, a crew of pickers in Harwich rebelled, went on a rampage and cut down seven cranberry forests. That looked like the end of the whole business. But a year later, someone passing one of the ruined areas saw pale green growth. The trees were coming back! As the trees grew tall, they were chopped back again. Once more, they produced fruit. They grew and were cut back still again.

Eventually, the once-famous cranberry trees were trained to grow low and dense, and pickers began working on their knees.

The cranberry bog, as we know it, is the practical result of the Picker Panic of 1837.

Visitors to the Nantucket Sound shore should learn to recognize and stay clear of the Crabapple Tree. This is a shrub-like tree that grows along the beach. It produces small, red-orange apples that nourish the Blue Crab. When high tide carries the crab in-shore, it scuttles to the Crabapple and fastens itself to the branches, eating all it can before the tide goes out.

Bathers walking barefoot should look sharp during this daily procession to and from the feeding areas.

The once-common Bayberry Tree is now a rare find on the Cape. The Bayberry grew only along the rim of Cape Cod Bay (hence the name BAYberry), primarily from the east end of Dennis to somewhere around the mid-section of Wellfleet. Great stands of these proud trees dotted the shoreline 100 years ago.

The new growth that springs upward from the end of each branch is called a "bayberry candle," and it was this unique feature that spelled doom for the Bayberry forests. In the latter part of the 19th century, it was a local custom to gather in the churchyard on Christmas Eve. Villagers went from there to the beach, lit the bayberry candles and formed circles around the flaming trees. According to a book of that time, "The carolers did sing sev'ral virses of suitable melodies, then proceeded homew'rd to the strains of 'Hey, Nonny-No and a Wassail Bowl.'" The trees were left to burn.

Shortly after the holiday, menfolk of the town would return and cut down what was left of the Bayberry. The remains were placed along the beach, where they helped hold the sand during winter storms and served as nesting areas for quahogs when they came ashore to lay their young.

Thus the Bayberry was used in many ways, but its numbers dwindled over the years. To find one now requires a sharp eye.

The same holds true for the Musseltoe.

Musseltoe was found in great abundance at one time. It grew low and thick in the locust swamps and sprouted deep blue berries about the size and shape of a thumb. Back in the days when families had jolly fun together, the Musseltoe was a source of great amusement.

Small sprigs of Musseltoe were hung in odd, out of the way places around the home and barn at just any time of year. Custom dictated that any small boy caught standing under the Musseltoe had to kiss a fat aunt and clean up around the goats. It was amusing for parents, but small boys—upon growing up—began to discontinue the practice. Sometime around the advent of talking pictures the Musseltoe sprigs had vanished altogether. In fact, throughout most of the swamps, those great clumps of the bush apparently had been destroyed.

The above information about musseltoe, cranberry forests and the like is just a smattering of all that is fascinating about Cape Cod. As you explore, you'll come to know more of its fauna, flora and history, not to mention the day-to-day life here. Feel free to ask local folks any questions you might have. Better still, ask the old-timers to tell you things that may have been left out of this book.

For instance, if you're down by the Coast Guard Station in Chatham, some helpful person may explain what they do with the Chatham Lighthouse when it's taken down for the winter.

And if you've noticed how the end of the Cape bends back toward Plymouth, you'll understand why the Pilgrim Monument was built in Provincetown. The largest granite structure in the country, the monument also is the tallest building on Cape Cod, and for good reason, too. In the old days, beginning about Memorial Day, spotters with telescopes were stationed at the top of the monument to count buggies and cars coming here from the mainland. This information, relayed to Scargo Tower in Dennis and then circulated around the towns, was of tremendous help when planning for summer business.

Finally, make sure someone tells you about the old car tunnel from Dennisport to Nantucket and what happened to it in World War II. That was a very sad day for all concerned.

SOME FINAL THOUGHTS
FROM ONE WHO LIVES HERE

The Company We Keep

Cape Cod, as we all know, has four seasons: Fall, Winter, Spring and Company. Fall is glorious, Winter, usually raw but snowless, Spring is three days in late April and Company is hot, blue-green and endless.

All of which brings to mind Labor Day Weekend of a few years past.

Undoubtedly, it was all my fault from the start. It was wrong of me to be born to parents who were open-hearted, generous of spirit and pretty easy about Company, no matter the inconvenience.

And it was a bad move on my part when, some months earlier, I began sharing a sprawly, quirky and beckoning house with a friend whose family crest bears the motto "Mi casa, su casa."

Mi casa had always been mi casa, and I was rather prickly about having guests unless they were entirely self-sufficient, never left the seat up, didn't expect actual food and had children who were not yet ambulatory. (See earlier reference to immobile infants.)

So it was with fear, loathing and one of those eye-squint headaches that I approached that summer's Grand Finale.

My friend—who had just moved to the Cape—had oodles of acquaintances from foreign countries, including England, California and Manhattan. Each of them said, "We'd love to see where you're living." (Hardly anybody says that if you've just moved to Yonkers.)

The list of arriving guests was pared down to the following: an actress from New York, two elderly gentlemen who had lived together for 43 years and a nun from California.

Then my best friend from college called. She'd been wanting me to meet her second husband. Naturally, I had met the first one, but he was no longer on the list of possible visitors. The only time they could come was—Labor Day Weekend. I said that we'd already booked a nun, an actress and two gay men, and oh, by the way, "We don't really have any beds yet."

This old friend (also of the mi casa, su casa persuasion and well-known for being more than willing to sleep in a broom closet) was undaunted. She thought it sounded like fun.

So we planned. I would move to the pull-out sofa in my study, the co-hostess would move to my room and give her own bed to the nun, who had been ill and shouldn't do the stairs. (I wasn't sure why we should be so shifted around for a nun, but then I'm Protestant.) My college pal would have the floor in the living room, and Husband II could have wherever he chose. (After meeting the nun, the men and the actress, he decided to sleep in the Volkswagen van.) The gents would be over the garage in two borrowed foldup cots, one of which apparently did just that during the night.

First off, because my co-hostess had a firm commitment elsewhere, I had to meet the nun at the airport. I'd never had practice spotting a nun in a crowd. What did one look for? Someone who looked cloistered? Untraveled? Catholic?

She was tall, tidy and had a vague look about the eyes. That should have tipped me off.

Once home, I got our guest settled in and unpacked. I suggested she rest up after her long flight, while I popped upstairs to finish an article due the next day.

About an hour later, I smelled smoke. Not the nice, barbecued pork kind of smoke, but something like fried electricity with metal sauce. I raced down the stairs to a smoke-filled living room and sleeping nun. I shook her awake, to learn that she had turned on the stove to make some tea, then left and dozed off.

I had—just the day before—gotten a set of those whimsical little burner covers—metal—with cows on them. Our guest had neglected to remove these, so the cow on the back left burner had melted and become part of the stove.

Our guest followed me to the kitchen and said, "Oh, my," which I gathered is what nuns say when they nearly burn down someone's house.

Later that afternoon, I left to run some errands, but not before tying Sister Flammable to a tree in the yard. When I got home, two strangers were sitting on the lawn having a drink. They called out their greetings and said, "We just love Molly!"

I didn't recognize these people and had never known a Molly, so I checked the house number to make sure I'd come to the right place.

Of course, they were the gentlemen from upstate New York, and Sister Incinerata had introduced my dog to them as "Molly." That her name was Amy didn't seem to matter. She called Amy "Molly" for two full weeks. (Did I mention that we thought she was coming for two days, but she said she said "weeks?")

Next came the actress. I loved her sight unseen,

because she insisted on staying at a bed and breakfast down the road near the beach. Her only requirement was cross-ventilation, probably because she lives in Manhattan where they don't have any.

She glided off the bus, wearing something diaphanous in a hundred shades of brown, a large foopy hat and eight or nine scarves, all wafting about her head. She simply adored everything she saw, not easy when you're heading east from Hyannis on Route 28.

Her room was so cross-ventilated that the wind off Nantucket Sound nearly blew her out the back window. She laughed at it all and went tripping down the road to do sand-dances on the beach. We blew kisses and tore home to check on Sister Inferno.

I all-but wept at the sight of my college friend, who had just arrived. She was familiar, comfortable and someone who would never play with the stove. She knelt to hug Amy, who was walking around in a fog, having lost her identity.

It all sifted down. We collected the actress, who was still burbling happily about how wonderful it all was, and took her back to the house where she burbled some more and took pictures of everything and everyone from every angle. The gents made us drinks, I fed "Molly," and we all sat in the yard listening to evening sounds. Much later, each of us found a bed, a vehicle or piece of floor, and all was silence.

What happens when you share a house on the Cape is that some rules must be made. No more than one guest or family unit at a time, to be mutually agreed upon in advance. No giving up of beds for visitors. No promise of large meals to be prepared by someone who doesn't like to cook. Nobody stays for two weeks.

And keep a fire extinguisher near the stove, in case of nuns.

The House

Down three roads and around two corners is a house that's been part of my life for most of my life. It's a summer house, which gives it a different shape and flavor and sound and smell than any house I've lived in.

I've been going to the house since my friend's grandfather owned it. He had a good smile and thick, shiny white hair. He sat in the second pew at church and said the blessing before dinner. That's what I remember about him. Children don't pay much attention to other people's grandfathers, which doesn't say much for children.

The house is old. Not antique, just old in ways that make it tilt and ramble. Floors go uphill or down. Doorways aren't quite on the square, and the too-narrow porch slants exactly enough to make you watch your step.

I've sat on that porch most of my Augusts in a gathering of summer friends I love. People driving by look to see who's sitting there, and we watch them watch us. I'm the only year-rounder, so I get to wave at somebody in a truck from time to time.

When dusk and mosquitoes arrive, we go inside and turn on lights.

The front room has two couches, a piano, a lamp and

not much else. The dining room is wall-to-wall table and mismatched chairs, and if your seat is on the north side, you have to go through two other rooms to reach it.

The living room—which probably was used for something else when the house was new—has a couch everyone vies for, odd chairs, a fireplace I'm not sure works and a bookcase. At summer's end, people leave what they finished reading and don't want to lug home.

There's a square oak table in the middle of the room, which seems a silly place for it, unless you want to do a puzzle or play a game or have dessert—in which case it's perfectly located. Next to the phone table is a chair that sticks out into the room just enough to be in the way of everyone carrying anything from the kitchen to the dining table or vice versa.

That kitchen is the color of French's mustard. A gas water heater in the corner snorts and woofs into action from time to time, and the two deep, white enamel sinks would be good places to bathe a pair of spaniels. The pantry is an explosion of mismatched dishes, pots, stacked canned goods, odd glasses, cold cereal and a shoeboxful of all the picks and crackers needed for eating lobster.

Upstairs is a sort of loaves-and-fishes situation; there are just enough bedrooms to go around, no matter how many are needed. They are little and littler, go this way and that off the hall and are full—always.

In the room behind the kitchen is a washer, and in the back yard is a clothesline where things flap and twist and get fog-damp or sun-dried: her shorts, his bathing suit, their towels and everybody's socks.

The house is at its best on late-summer nights, when out of open windows all around spill supper smells, laughter, conversation from the dishwashing team, talk between friends and the occasional Chopin from the old upright.

And then it's over. Wicker chairs are stacked in the front hall. The water heater stops woofing. Windows are locked tight, all is unplugged and the last car pulls away.

I drive by often in the winter—just to make sure of the old place.

It's not my house.

But it's in my life.

The Food

Not long ago, I had the anticipatory, pre-Labor Day, All-My-Summer-Friends-Are-Leaving, What'll-I-Do blues. It happens every year. Everyone goes, and I drive past shuttered houses, nothing to look forward to but raking leaves, putting away lawn furniture and draining garden hoses.

On the other hand, there's a positive side to this. When your summer friends go, they give you their food. You have to take it all, because they're leaving at 4 a.m. and can't go to the dump. So you lug it home, sort it out and pass along whatever you can't stand. It's post-season recycling.

What is it that people leave behind?

Nothing really good.

I've never gotten a package of Pepperidge Farm cookies, for example, or a bag of hazlenut coffee. I'm not sure I've ever said, "Oh, great. I need that. I just ran out!"

What they leave is a part of this and the rest of those and everything from the refrigerator door. Their door stuff moves to my door and stays for two or three years. I don't get to pass it on, because I never go away.

Door stuff is what you buy because you need it once. Maybe twice. But you never use it all. Ketchup. Or catsup. I get ketchup every Labor Day. And mustard. Stone

95

ground. Honey. Guilden's. French's. Hot. Onion garlic. And I get three bottles with two inches each of Caesar, Italian, Lite Creamy Ranch and pseudo-Blue Cheese salad dressing. One half-bottle of cocktail sauce and some RealLemon Juice. I don't know what that's for, but I have some.

People also leave what they bought for someone else, but someone else was there for only three days. So I get Cap'n Crunch Cereal, diet Dr. Pepper and mint jelly. (Edna did a lamb roast last Tuesday.)

Finally, they leave what they're pretty sure won't survive the trip home. Meat. Mayo. Those bananas might make it, but they won't be pretty, so do you want them?

Here's what I got when my friends left for Ohio (on balance, it was better than what the Michigan group left, but not quite as appealing as the Washington, D.C. remains of the day): in addition to ketchupmustardsaladdressingmintjelly, a part bag of potatoes, a box of grated parmesan cheese (from the door), feta cheese (door), baby gherkins (door), six small eggs and a pound of Ballpark Beef Franks (I just ran out!). Five cans of 7-Up. (The only thing I like less than 7-Up is Dr. Pepper.) Boxes of angel hair pasta, Minute Rice and sugar. A bag of flour. (I don't use my flour much. Every few months I check to see if it, you know, wiggles.) Four of those little individual boxes of cereal: two Frosted Flakes and two Fruit Loops. (I'll have that with some Dr. Pepper.) Seven cans of diet, sweetened, natural lemon-flavored iced tea, whatever that is. Ten onions. TEN. Based on my average use, I'll have onions until March 3.

This whole thing could be better organized. Winter people who know summer people ought to write down names and begin making phone calls in, say, mid-August. Plan the route. Bring boxes. With enough stops, you could be stocked up until early November.

But the mint jelly goes to the dump.

The Last Word

It's been suggested that this book end with a complete list of rules for both hosts and guests. That's not a bad idea.

The list is as follows:

Do unto others
as you would have others do unto you.

Favorite Places

Restaurants

People

Addresses & Phone Numbers

Marcia J. Monbleau is not a native Cape Codder, having moved here when she was 11. Like most Cape teens, she did not spend her summers lollygagging, but was a waitress, chambermaid and a soda jerk at her brother's 5&10. Now more or less grown up, she has been a long-time newspaper reporter and feature editor, publicity director at The Cape Playhouse in Dennis, host and executive producer of tv's "Offstage" and has written several books, most of them about the people and history of Cape Cod. She lives in Harwich Port, where, from time to time, she has company.

Other books by the author:
Ingenious Inventions
At Home—Harwich
The Cape Playhouse
Home Song—Chatham
Pleasant Bay—Stories from a Cape Cod Place
To Always Persevere: The Diaries of Benjamin Franklin Robbins
A Home on the Rolling Deep—Stories of Chatham Sea Captains

Lucretia Romey is a painter, illustrator, quilter, teacher and close observer of the natural world. She lives in Orleans in an old house with steep stairs, scatter rugs, an occasional earwig and the inevitable guests.